To Ruth
Happy Bi...
Lo...

SCATTY

SCATTY

BRITISH CATS, FRENCH CATS

& COSMOPOLITAN CATS

BY

MAX REINHARDT

LONDON

© Siné 1958, 1977
ISBN 0 370 30046 7
Printed in Great Britain for
Max Reinhardt Ltd
9 Bow Street, London WC2E 7AL
by William Clowes & Sons, Limited
First published 1958
First published in this format 1977

BRITISH
CATS

Lord Kit chener

provo cat ive

intoxi cat e

sophisti cat e

deli cat e

cat alogue

cat's whiskers

domestic cat

cat erwaul

se cat eurs

cat's pyjama

cat nap

deli cat essen

cat e gory

fraidy cat

cat on hot bricks

cat apult

hell cat

mus cat el

cat holic

cat echism

pizzi cat o

toc cat a

cat gut

hep cats

cat fish

cat amaran

octo puss

cats and dogs

cat arrh

s cat

cat's cradle

cat erpillar

cat er pillar (2)

cat erpillar (3)

dupli cat e

tripli cat e

quadrupli cat e

con cat enation

desic cat e

cat aract

suffo cat e

cat's paw

cat a lyst

cat hode

cat call

catty corner

cat alepsy

copy cat

Pus illanimous

intri cat e

cat nip

trun cat e

cat o nine tails

cat as trophe

Requies cat

FRENCH
CATS

entre-chat

chat monisc

chat cha cha

chat peron

chat teau

chat sœur

chat steté

chat rité

chat teaubriant

chat let d'aisance

chat peau

COSMOPOLITAN
CATS

Lady Chat terley...

Eartha Kitt

.. et son garde-chat sse

Coco Chat nel

Chat plin

Chat s'Addams

Chat gall

Cat ullus (84-47 B.C.)

Chat rlemagne

Cat herine the Great

Chat kespeare

G. B. Chat

Œdi puss

Œdi puss complex

Ror chat k

platy puss

cat on a hot tin roof

pole cat

Cat chat turian

Chat liapine

gei chat

Siamese cat

pa chat

Cat alan

Chat lom

In chat lah

Kitty Hawk

Chat tanooga choo choo

He cat e

the Owl and the Pussy Cat

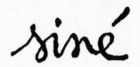

Siné was born in Paris in 1928. After training as a typographer, he was so impressed by his first sight of the work of Steinberg that he immediately began drawing cartoons himself. He succeeded brilliantly, and has never looked back. He is France's best-known political cartoonist, and he has worked in every medium from newspapers and books to stage décor and films.